Table Of Contents

Chapter 1: Introduction to Generative AI in Education

Defining Generative AI

Generative AI refers to a category of artificial intelligence that focuses on creating new content, ideas, or solutions by leveraging algorithms and vast datasets. This technology uses machine learning models, particularly deep learning techniques, to generate outputs that mimic human-like creativity. In the context of education, generative AI can produce a wide array of materials, including personalized learning resources, assessments, and interactive simulations, which can enhance the educational experience for students. As educators, administrators, and researchers navigate this evolving landscape, understanding the foundational principles of generative AI is essential for effectively integrating it into educational settings.

One of the most significant applications of generative AI in education is in the development of AI-powered tutoring systems. These systems harness the capabilities of generative AI to tailor learning experiences to individual student needs. By analyzing student performance data and learning preferences, AI-powered tutors can generate customized exercises, feedback, and instructional content that align with each learner's unique requirements. This personalized approach not only enhances engagement but also allows students to progress at their own pace, ultimately leading to improved academic outcomes.

Moreover, the integration of virtual reality (VR) and generative AI in classrooms offers transformative opportunities for immersive learning experiences. By combining VR environments with generative AI, educators can create dynamic simulations that adapt in real-time based on student interactions. For example, a history lesson could be transformed into an interactive experience where students explore ancient civilizations in a virtual setting, guided by AI-generated narratives that respond to their inquiries. This synergy between VR and generative AI enables richer, more engaging learning experiences that can deepen students' understanding of complex concepts.

As the adoption of generative AI in education grows, it also raises important ethical considerations and policy implications. Educators and administrators must carefully evaluate the potential biases embedded in AI algorithms, as well as the implications of data privacy and security. Ensuring that AI tools are used responsibly and equitably is critical for fostering an inclusive educational environment. Discussions around AI ethics and policy must be at the forefront of conversations among stakeholders in education to establish guidelines that prioritize student welfare and uphold academic integrity.

Lastly, collaborative learning platforms that utilize generative AI can revolutionize the way students interact and collaborate on projects. These platforms can facilitate peer-to-peer learning by generating discussion prompts, project ideas, and resources tailored to group dynamics and individual contributions. By leveraging generative AI, educators can create environments that promote teamwork, critical thinking, and creativity. As research continues to explore the efficacy of these platforms, it becomes increasingly clear that generative AI holds the potential to redefine collaborative learning by making it more accessible, engaging, and effective for diverse student populations.

The Evolution of Educational Technologies

The evolution of educational technologies has undergone significant transformations, particularly with the advent of generative AI. Early educational technologies primarily focused on delivering content through static media such as textbooks and slideshows. As computer technology advanced, the introduction of multimedia resources enabled a more interactive learning experience. Educational software began to incorporate basic adaptive learning systems that catered to individual learning paces, setting the stage for the development of more sophisticated AI-powered tutoring systems. This foundational shift laid the groundwork for the integration of advanced AI capabilities, including personalized learning pathways and real-time feedback mechanisms.

The emergence of AI in education has revolutionized how students engage with learning materials. AI-powered tutoring systems have developed from simple question-and-answer interfaces to complex algorithms capable of analyzing student performance in real-time. These systems can adapt to individual learning styles and needs, providing tailored support that enhances student comprehension and retention. Such technologies not only foster a more engaging learning environment but also allow educators to focus on facilitating discussions and collaborative learning experiences rather than merely delivering content. This shift represents a significant move toward a more personalized educational approach, where technology acts as a partner in the learning process.

Virtual reality (VR) has also played a crucial role in the evolution of educational technologies. By creating immersive learning environments, VR allows students to engage with complex concepts in a hands-on manner. When integrated with AI, VR can simulate real-world scenarios, providing learners with interactive experiences that deepen understanding and retention. For instance, students can explore historical sites, conduct virtual science experiments, or practice language skills in culturally relevant contexts. This integration not only enhances the learning experience but also prepares students for the demands of an increasingly digital and interconnected world.

As these technologies continue to evolve, ethical considerations and policy frameworks surrounding AI in education have become paramount. Educators and administrators must navigate the implications of data privacy, algorithmic bias, and equitable access to AI-driven resources. Developing policies that ensure responsible use of AI in educational settings is critical to fostering an environment where all students can benefit from these innovations. It is essential for stakeholders in education to engage in discussions about the ethical dimensions of AI, ensuring that technology serves to enhance, rather than hinder, educational equity.

Collaborative learning platforms that utilize AI are emerging as powerful tools for fostering teamwork and communication among students. These platforms leverage AI to facilitate group interactions, enabling learners to collaborate on projects, share resources, and provide peer feedback. By analyzing group dynamics and individual contributions, AI can help educators identify areas for improvement and support the development of essential collaborative skills. As educational technologies continue to evolve, the role of AI in promoting collaborative learning will be increasingly important, driving engagement and enhancing the overall educational experience for students in diverse learning environments.

The Role of AI in Modern Education

The integration of artificial intelligence (AI) into modern education has fundamentally transformed teaching methodologies and learning experiences. AI-powered tools are being utilized to create personalized learning paths, allowing educators to tailor their instruction to meet the diverse needs of students. With the capacity to analyze vast amounts of data, AI systems can identify individual learning styles, preferences, and progress, thus enabling customized feedback and resources. This level of personalization not only enhances student engagement but also fosters a more inclusive learning environment where every student can thrive.

AI-powered tutoring systems have emerged as a powerful complement to traditional classroom instruction. These systems provide students with on-demand support, offering explanations, practice problems, and feedback at their convenience. By harnessing machine learning algorithms, these platforms can adapt to each student's unique learning pace, ensuring that they receive the assistance they need when they need it. This immediate access to help can significantly reduce frustration and learning gaps, ultimately contributing to improved academic performance. Educators can leverage these systems to enhance their teaching without diminishing their role as facilitators of learning.

The incorporation of virtual reality (VR) and AI in classrooms represents a significant leap in educational technology. VR environments, enhanced by AI capabilities, can simulate real-world scenarios that allow students to immerse themselves in complex subjects, from historical events to scientific experiments. This experiential learning approach not only captures students' attention but also promotes critical thinking and problem-solving skills. By engaging with content in a dynamic and interactive way, students can develop a deeper understanding of the material, thus enhancing retention and application of knowledge.

As AI continues to permeate educational settings, ethical considerations and policy frameworks must be carefully examined. The deployment of AI technologies raises questions about data privacy, algorithmic bias, and equitable access to these resources. Educators, administrators, and researchers must collaborate to establish guidelines that ensure AI's use in education is fair and transparent. This involves creating policies that protect student data while promoting ethical AI practices, ultimately fostering a safe and supportive environment for all learners. Engaging in dialogue about these issues is essential to navigate the complexities of AI integration responsibly.

Collaborative learning platforms utilizing AI are also reshaping the educational landscape by facilitating peer-to-peer interaction and knowledge sharing. These platforms harness AI to connect students based on shared interests, learning goals, or complementary skills, fostering a sense of community and collaboration. By encouraging students to work together on projects or discussions, these platforms enhance social learning and critical thinking. Educators can harness the power of these AI-driven tools to create collaborative experiences that prepare students for the interconnected world they will face beyond the classroom, equipping them with essential skills for the future.

Chapter 2: AI-Powered Tutoring Systems

Overview of AI Tutoring Systems

AI tutoring systems represent a transformative approach to personalized education, leveraging advanced algorithms and machine learning techniques to provide tailored learning experiences. These systems are designed to adapt to individual student needs, learning styles, and performance levels. By analyzing data from student interactions, AI tutoring systems can identify strengths and weaknesses, offering customized feedback and resources that enhance understanding and retention of material. This adaptability makes them a valuable tool for educators seeking to address the diverse needs of their students in increasingly heterogeneous classrooms.

The architecture of AI tutoring systems often incorporates natural language processing, enabling them to engage in meaningful conversations with students. This interaction not only helps clarify concepts but also fosters a sense of connection that can be crucial for student motivation. Additionally, these systems can integrate with existing educational platforms, allowing for a seamless blend of traditional teaching methods with AI-driven insights. Educators can utilize these systems to augment their teaching strategies, providing a hybrid model that combines direct instruction with personalized support.

Incorporating AI tutoring systems into classroom settings encourages collaborative learning experiences. These systems can facilitate group projects by analyzing the dynamics of student interactions and suggesting optimal team configurations. By promoting collaborative problem-solving, AI tutoring systems can enhance critical thinking and communication skills among students. This synergy between AI technology and collaborative learning fosters an environment where students can engage meaningfully with their peers while benefiting from the support of AI-driven insights.

However, the implementation of AI tutoring systems also raises important ethical considerations. Issues of data privacy, algorithmic bias, and the potential for over-reliance on technology are critical discussions among educators and policymakers. As AI systems collect and analyze large amounts of student data, it is crucial to establish clear guidelines and policies that protect student information while ensuring equitable access to AI resources. Educators must navigate these ethical landscapes to ensure that the integration of AI in education serves to enhance learning rather than inadvertently reinforce existing disparities.

The future of AI tutoring systems in education is promising, particularly as advancements in generative AI continue to evolve. As these technologies become more sophisticated, they are likely to offer even more nuanced insights into student learning processes. Educators, administrators, and researchers must remain engaged in ongoing discussions about AI's role in education, exploring its potential to foster innovation, improve educational outcomes, and create equitable learning opportunities. By embracing AI tutoring systems, the educational landscape can be revolutionized, paving the way for a more personalized, efficient, and engaging learning environment for all students.

Personalization and Adaptivity in Learning

Personalization and adaptivity in learning are critical components in the evolution of educational environments, especially with the integration of generative AI technologies. Traditional educational models often adopt a one-size-fits-all approach, which can overlook the unique learning needs and preferences of individual students. Generative AI has the potential to transform this landscape by tailoring educational experiences to align with each learner's capabilities, interests, and learning pace. This capability not only enhances engagement but also promotes deeper understanding and retention of knowledge.

AI-powered tutoring systems are a prime example of how personalization can be achieved in educational settings. These systems utilize algorithms that analyze a student's performance in real-time, adapting the content and delivery methods accordingly. By assessing a learner's strengths and weaknesses, AI tutors can provide customized feedback, suggest resources, and adjust the difficulty of tasks to better suit the individual. This dynamic interaction fosters a more personalized educational journey, allowing students to progress at their own pace and build confidence in their abilities.

Moreover, the integration of virtual reality with AI can further enhance personalized learning experiences. VR environments can be designed to adapt in real-time, responding to a student's actions and decisions to create immersive scenarios that facilitate experiential learning. For example, in a science class, a virtual lab can present challenges that adjust based on a student's previous interactions, ensuring that learners remain engaged and challenged without feeling overwhelmed. This level of adaptivity allows for exploration and experimentation in a safe setting, encouraging curiosity and critical thinking.

However, the implementation of personalization and adaptivity through generative AI also raises important ethical considerations. Educators and administrators must ensure that the data collected from students is handled responsibly, protecting privacy and maintaining transparency in how information is used. Additionally, there is a need for policies that guide the ethical use of AI in educational contexts, ensuring that all students benefit equally from these advancements. Addressing these ethical concerns is crucial to fostering trust among stakeholders and promoting equitable access to personalized learning experiences.

Finally, collaborative learning platforms utilizing AI can further support personalized and adaptive education. These platforms can facilitate group work and peer-to-peer interactions, allowing students to learn from one another while still receiving individualized support. AI can analyze group dynamics and suggest optimal collaboration strategies, ensuring that each student's voice is heard and valued. By creating an environment where personalized learning intersects with collaborative efforts, educators can cultivate a more holistic and inclusive educational experience that prepares students for the complexities of the modern world.

Case Studies of Successful AI Tutoring Implementations

The integration of AI tutoring systems in educational settings has led to significant advancements in personalized learning experiences. One notable case study is the implementation of an AI-powered tutoring system at a large urban high school in California. This system, which leverages generative AI algorithms, was designed to adapt to individual student learning styles and needs. Following its introduction, data revealed a 20% increase in student engagement and a marked improvement in overall academic performance. Educators noted that students who previously struggled with traditional learning methods found renewed motivation and success through tailored support, highlighting the profound impact of AI on student outcomes.

Another compelling example comes from a rural school district in Texas that integrated AI tutoring alongside virtual reality (VR) to enhance STEM education. By combining these technologies, students were able to explore complex scientific concepts in immersive environments while receiving real-time feedback from an AI tutor. The results were remarkable: students reported a 30% increase in their understanding of the material, and assessments showed improved test scores in physics and chemistry. This case emphasizes how the synergy between AI and VR not only engages students but also deepens their comprehension of challenging subjects, showcasing the potential for innovative teaching methods.

In a different context, a private university on the East Coast adopted a collaborative learning platform that utilized AI to facilitate peer tutoring among students. This platform matched students based on their strengths and weaknesses, allowing them to teach and learn from one another under the guidance of an AI system. The initiative led to a 15% rise in retention rates among first-year students, as the collaborative nature of the learning environment fostered a sense of community and support. This case study illustrates the effectiveness of AI in promoting collaborative learning, emphasizing the importance of social interaction in educational success.

Moreover, the ethical implications of AI in education cannot be overlooked. A case study from a prominent research university examined the implementation of an AI tutoring system that emphasized transparency and data privacy. The institution worked closely with AI ethicists to ensure that student data was handled responsibly and that the AI's decision-making processes were understandable to both educators and students. This careful consideration of ethics in the deployment of technology not only built trust among users but also served as a model for best practices in AI integration in educational settings.

Finally, an international project focused on AI-powered tutoring across multiple countries provided valuable insights into cultural adaptability. The project involved developing AI systems that could cater to diverse educational contexts and curricula. Educators involved reported that the AI's ability to adapt to local languages and learning standards was crucial for its acceptance and effectiveness. As a result, students from various backgrounds benefited from personalized educational support that resonated with their individual learning environments. This case underscores the necessity of considering cultural contexts in AI implementations, ensuring that technology enhances educational experiences globally.

Chapter 3: Virtual Reality and AI Integration in Classrooms

Understanding Virtual Reality in Education

Virtual reality (VR) in education offers immersive experiences that can significantly enhance learning outcomes. By creating interactive and engaging environments, VR allows students to explore complex concepts in ways that traditional methods cannot. Educators can utilize VR to simulate real-world scenarios, enabling students to practice skills in a safe and controlled setting. For instance, medical students can participate in virtual surgeries, while history students can experience historical events firsthand. This technology not only increases engagement but also caters to diverse learning styles, making education more accessible to all students.

Incorporating VR into the curriculum presents unique opportunities for collaboration among educators, administrators, and researchers. By working together, they can develop VR content tailored to specific educational goals. Such collaboration can lead to the creation of shared resources, which can be used across various institutions. Researchers can study the effectiveness of VR in different educational contexts, providing valuable insights into best practices and potential pitfalls. This collective approach ensures that VR is not merely an add-on but an integral part of a comprehensive educational strategy.

Integrating AI with VR further amplifies the potential of these technologies in educational settings. AI-powered tutoring systems can adapt to individual student needs while providing real-time feedback within a VR environment. This combination allows for personalized learning experiences where students can progress at their own pace. AI can also analyze student interactions within the VR space, offering insights that can inform instructional strategies. By leveraging AI, educators can ensure that VR applications are not only engaging but also effective in promoting deeper understanding and retention of knowledge.

While the benefits of VR in education are significant, it is essential to consider the ethical implications of its integration. Issues such as data privacy, student consent, and the potential for misuse of VR technologies must be addressed. Educators and administrators must develop policies that protect students while fostering innovation. Establishing ethical guidelines will help ensure that VR is used responsibly and equitably, preventing disparities in access and learning opportunities. Engaging in discussions about AI ethics and policy will be crucial as these technologies continue to evolve.

Finally, the future of VR in education will likely be shaped by ongoing advancements in technology and pedagogy. As VR becomes more accessible and affordable, its integration into classrooms will likely increase. Educators must remain informed about the latest developments in both VR and AI to effectively harness these tools for enhanced learning experiences. Continuous professional development and collaboration among educators will be vital to navigate this rapidly changing landscape. By understanding and embracing VR in education, stakeholders can create enriched learning environments that prepare students for a future where technology plays an increasingly central role.

Enhancing Learning Experiences with AI and VR

The integration of Artificial Intelligence (AI) and Virtual Reality (VR) in education holds transformative potential for enhancing learning experiences. AI-powered tools can analyze student performance in real time, allowing for personalized learning pathways that cater to individual needs and preferences. These tools can identify strengths and weaknesses, enabling educators to tailor their teaching strategies effectively. Furthermore, AI-powered tutoring systems can provide instant feedback and support, ensuring that learners receive the guidance they need precisely when they need it. This individualized approach not only fosters student engagement but also promotes a deeper understanding of the material.

Virtual Reality, when combined with AI, creates immersive learning environments that simulate real-world scenarios. By enabling students to explore complex concepts in a safe and controlled setting, VR can enhance experiential learning. For instance, students can virtually visit historical sites, conduct science experiments, or even practice medical procedures without the risks associated with real-life applications. This immersive experience can significantly increase retention and comprehension, as learners are able to visualize and interact with the subject matter in ways that traditional learning methods cannot achieve. The unique combination of AI's adaptability and VR's immersive qualities can redefine how educators approach curriculum design and instructional delivery.

Collaborative learning platforms utilizing AI further enhance the educational experience by fostering peer interaction and cooperative learning. These platforms can facilitate group projects and discussions, enabling students to collaborate across geographical boundaries. AI can assist in forming diverse groups based on individual strengths, interests, and learning styles, promoting a richer collaborative environment. By incorporating features such as real-time feedback and adaptive content, these platforms can guide students through group dynamics, ensuring effective communication and teamwork. This approach not only prepares students for the collaborative nature of the modern workforce but also cultivates essential interpersonal skills.

While the benefits of AI and VR in education are significant, it is crucial to address the ethical implications and policy considerations surrounding their implementation. Educators, administrators, and researchers must prioritize data privacy and security as they integrate these technologies into educational settings. Establishing clear guidelines and ethical standards will be essential in ensuring that student data is protected and used responsibly. Furthermore, equitable access to AI and VR resources must be a priority to prevent widening the digital divide. As these technologies become more prevalent, ongoing discussions about their ethical implications will be vital in shaping policies that foster inclusive and responsible educational environments.

In conclusion, the synergy of AI and VR offers a promising frontier for enhancing learning experiences in education. By leveraging AI's analytical capabilities and VR's immersive environments, educators can create dynamic and personalized learning experiences that engage students more deeply. The potential for collaborative learning and innovative instructional strategies can reshape the educational landscape, but it is essential to navigate the ethical considerations with care. As educators, administrators, and researchers embrace these technologies, a commitment to responsible use will ensure that the benefits are realized across diverse educational contexts.

Examples of AI-Driven VR Educational Programs

AI-driven virtual reality (VR) educational programs are transforming the landscape of learning by creating immersive experiences that engage students in unique ways. One notable example is "Engage," a platform that allows educators to build and share interactive VR lessons. By integrating artificial intelligence, Engage personalizes the learning experience based on individual student needs and progress. This adaptability ensures that learners can explore topics at their own pace, making the educational process more effective and enjoyable. Educators can create simulations that mimic real-world scenarios, enhancing comprehension and retention of complex concepts.

Another compelling example is "Immerse," which focuses on language learning through VR environments. This program utilizes AI to assess students' language proficiency and tailor exercises accordingly. Through realistic simulations, learners practice speaking and listening in contextual environments, such as ordering food in a restaurant or conducting a business meeting. The AI component analyzes student performance, providing feedback and adjusting difficulty levels in real-time. This method not only promotes language acquisition but also builds confidence in students as they engage in practical applications of their skills.

"Labster" represents a pioneering approach to science education through virtual reality. This platform offers VR labs that allow students to conduct experiments in a safe and controlled environment. AI algorithms analyze students' actions and decisions within the lab, offering hints and guidance when needed. This hands-on learning experience is particularly beneficial in subjects like chemistry and biology, where access to physical labs can be limited. By simulating real-life scientific processes, Labster enhances conceptual understanding and fosters a genuine interest in STEM fields.

The "ClassVR" platform is another example of how AI and VR can enhance collaborative learning. ClassVR provides educators with a library of immersive experiences that can be used to facilitate group discussions and teamwork among students. The AI component tracks student interactions and engagement levels, helping teachers identify dynamics within groups and adjust their teaching strategies accordingly. This approach not only promotes collaboration but also encourages critical thinking and problem-solving skills, essential competencies in today's educational landscape.

Finally, the "VR Classroom" initiative exemplifies the integration of AI and VR for remote learning environments. This program creates virtual classrooms where students can interact with peers and instructors from around the world. AI-driven features include automated attendance, real-time language translation, and personalized learning pathways based on student performance. Such initiatives address the challenges of traditional online education by providing a more engaging and interactive experience, which is crucial for maintaining student motivation and participation. As these examples illustrate, AI-driven VR educational programs are at the forefront of revolutionizing how education is delivered and experienced, paving the way for innovative learning solutions in diverse educational settings.

Chapter 4: AI Ethics and Policy in Education

The Importance of Ethics in AI

The integration of artificial intelligence (AI) into educational settings has brought numerous advantages, yet it has also raised critical ethical considerations that must be addressed. Ethics in AI is particularly important in education because the decisions made by AI systems can significantly impact students' learning experiences, privacy, and overall well-being. Educators, administrators, and researchers must recognize that the deployment of AI technologies in classrooms is not merely a technical endeavor; it is also a moral one that demands careful consideration of the implications of these technologies on learners and educators alike.

One of the primary ethical concerns surrounding AI in education is the issue of data privacy. AI-powered systems often rely on vast amounts of student data to function effectively. This data may include personal information, academic performance, and behavioral patterns. It is essential that educators and administrators prioritize the protection of students' privacy by implementing robust data governance policies. Clear guidelines should be established regarding data collection, usage, and storage to ensure that students' rights are respected and that their information is not misused. Educators must advocate for transparent practices that build trust between AI developers, educational institutions, and the students they serve.

Another critical aspect of ethics in AI is the potential for bias in AI algorithms. If the data used to train these systems is not representative or is embedded with biases, the AI can perpetuate and even exacerbate existing inequalities in education. For instance, biased algorithms may lead to unfair assessments of students' capabilities or unfair resource allocation. Educators and researchers must work collaboratively to identify and mitigate these biases by diversifying data sources and employing ethical AI frameworks. This proactive approach will ensure that AI systems support equitable learning opportunities for all students, regardless of their backgrounds.

Furthermore, the role of AI in shaping educational policies cannot be overlooked. As AI technologies become more ingrained in the educational landscape, policymakers must consider the ethical implications of their use. This includes developing regulations that ensure accountability for AI-driven decisions made in educational settings. Educators and administrators are crucial in advocating for policies that not only promote innovation but also safeguard ethical standards. Engaging in discussions about AI ethics can help create a balanced approach that prioritizes educational equity and student welfare.

Lastly, fostering a culture of ethical awareness among educators and students is imperative for the responsible use of AI in education. Professional development programs should include training on AI ethics, enabling educators to critically assess the technologies they implement in their classrooms. Additionally, students should be educated about the ethical implications of AI, empowering them to navigate an increasingly AI-driven world with informed perspectives. By embedding ethical considerations into the educational discourse, stakeholders can cultivate an environment where AI enhances learning experiences while upholding the fundamental values of integrity and respect.

Data Privacy Concerns in Educational AI

The integration of artificial intelligence in education has sparked a myriad of advancements, yet it has also raised significant concerns regarding data privacy. As educational institutions increasingly adopt AI-powered tools and platforms, the collection, storage, and use of student data become paramount issues. These systems are designed to tailor learning experiences, enhance engagement, and provide personalized feedback, but they often require extensive data inputs from students. This reliance on data can lead to vulnerabilities, potentially exposing sensitive information and violating privacy regulations.

One of the primary concerns revolves around the collection of personally identifiable information (PII). Educational AI systems often gather data such as names, addresses, academic performance, and behavioral patterns to function effectively. While this data can improve learning outcomes, it also creates risks if not managed properly. Instances of data breaches in educational settings have highlighted the dangers of inadequate security measures. It is crucial for educators and administrators to understand the implications of data collection practices and to implement robust security protocols to protect student information.

Another aspect of data privacy in educational AI involves compliance with regulations such as the Family Educational Rights and Privacy Act (FERPA) and the General Data Protection Regulation (GDPR). These laws are designed to safeguard student data, but the rapidly evolving nature of AI technology often outpaces legislative measures. Educators and institutions must stay informed about legal requirements and ensure that AI tools they utilize comply with these regulations. Failure to do so could lead to legal repercussions and a loss of trust among students and parents.

In addition to legal compliance, ethical considerations play a significant role in data privacy concerns. The use of AI in education raises questions about consent and transparency. Students and their guardians should be informed about what data is collected, how it will be used, and who will have access to it. Building trust is essential in fostering a positive learning environment, and transparency in data practices is a vital component of this trust. Educators and administrators need to prioritize ethical guidelines that promote responsible data handling and empower students with knowledge about their own data rights.

Finally, addressing data privacy concerns in educational AI requires a collaborative approach among stakeholders, including educators, administrators, policymakers, and technology developers. By working together, these groups can establish best practices and frameworks that prioritize student privacy while still harnessing the benefits of AI in education. Continuous dialogue about the ethical implications of AI technologies will help create a more secure and trustworthy educational landscape, enabling the effective use of AI tools without compromising student data integrity.

Developing Policies for Responsible AI Use in Education

The integration of generative AI technologies in educational settings presents both opportunities and challenges that necessitate the development of comprehensive policies for responsible use. Educators, administrators, and researchers must prioritize the establishment of guidelines that address ethical considerations, data privacy, and equitable access to AI resources. These policies should aim to foster a safe and inclusive learning environment where AI enhances educational experiences while safeguarding the interests of all stakeholders.

One critical aspect of these policies is the ethical use of AI-powered tutoring systems. These systems can provide personalized learning experiences, but they must be designed to avoid biases and ensure fairness. Policies should mandate transparency in how AI algorithms operate, allowing educators to understand the decision-making processes behind personalized recommendations. This transparency can help build trust among students and parents, ensuring that AI serves as a supportive tool rather than a source of discrimination or inequality.

Data privacy is another essential consideration in the development of AI policies. With the increasing reliance on AI in education, safeguarding student data becomes paramount. Policies must establish clear standards for data collection, storage, and usage, ensuring compliance with legal regulations such as FERPA and GDPR. Additionally, educators should be trained on best practices for managing student data, fostering a culture of responsibility that prioritizes the confidentiality and security of sensitive information.

Equitable access to AI resources is vital for maximizing the benefits of generative AI in education. Policies should address the digital divide, ensuring that all students, regardless of their socio-economic background, have access to AI tools and technologies. This includes investing in infrastructure, providing training for educators, and offering resources that help integrate AI into various learning environments. By promoting equitable access, educational institutions can harness the potential of AI to enhance learning outcomes for diverse student populations.

Finally, fostering collaborative learning platforms that utilize AI requires policies that encourage innovation while maintaining ethical standards. Educators and administrators must facilitate collaboration among stakeholders, including technology developers, to create AI tools that align with educational goals. This collaboration can lead to the development of AI systems that not only enhance learning experiences but also empower students to engage critically with technology. By embracing a responsible approach to AI policy development, the educational sector can ensure that generative AI serves as a transformative force that enriches learning for all.

Chapter 5: Collaborative Learning Platforms Utilizing AI

The Rise of Collaborative Learning

The rise of collaborative learning has been significantly influenced by advancements in technology, particularly through the integration of generative AI. This approach emphasizes the importance of social interaction and teamwork in the educational process, allowing learners to engage more deeply with content and with one another. Collaborative learning platforms utilize AI to facilitate group projects, peer feedback, and shared problem-solving, fostering an environment where students can co-create knowledge. By leveraging generative AI, educators can design experiences that not only adapt to individual learning styles but also promote teamwork, critical thinking, and communication skills.

Generative AI-powered tutoring systems are a prime example of how technology can enhance collaborative learning. These systems analyze student interactions and provide tailored support that encourages collaboration among peers. For instance, AI can identify when students are struggling with specific concepts and recommend forming groups with complementary skills. This targeted approach not only helps students grasp difficult topics but also encourages them to work together, thereby fostering a sense of community and shared responsibility for learning outcomes. As students collaborate, they learn to appreciate diverse perspectives, which is a crucial skill in today's interconnected world.

Virtual reality (VR) and AI integration in classrooms have also played a pivotal role in the rise of collaborative learning. VR environments can immerse students in realistic scenarios that require teamwork to navigate challenges and solve problems. AI enhances this experience by personalizing the virtual environment based on the group dynamics and individual contributions. For example, AI can monitor student interactions and suggest roles or tasks within a virtual team, ensuring that all members are engaged and contributing. This dynamic not only enriches the learning experience but also prepares students for real-world collaboration in diverse settings.

In the context of AI ethics and policy, the rise of collaborative learning necessitates a careful consideration of how these technologies are implemented. As educators and administrators adopt AI-driven collaborative platforms, they must ensure that ethical guidelines are established to protect student data and promote fairness. Transparency in how AI algorithms function and the data they utilize is vital to maintaining trust among students and educators. Furthermore, discussions surrounding accessibility and equity in AI use must be prioritized to ensure that all students can benefit from collaborative learning opportunities, regardless of their backgrounds.

Looking forward, the ongoing evolution of collaborative learning, bolstered by generative AI, presents exciting possibilities for the future of education. As these technologies continue to develop, educators, administrators, and researchers will need to stay informed about the latest advancements and best practices. By embracing collaborative learning powered by AI, the educational community can create more inclusive, adaptive, and engaging environments that prepare students for the complexities of the modern world. The challenges of implementation and ethical considerations will require ongoing dialogue, but the potential benefits for student engagement and learning outcomes are profound.

AI Tools for Enhancing Collaboration

AI tools are transforming collaboration in educational settings, providing new avenues for educators, administrators, and researchers to enhance learning experiences. Collaborative learning platforms powered by AI facilitate real-time interaction among students and educators, breaking down traditional barriers to communication. These platforms utilize natural language processing and machine learning algorithms to tailor discussions and group activities based on individual learning styles and needs. As a result, educators can create more inclusive environments where diverse voices contribute to collective knowledge construction.

AI-powered tutoring systems are another significant advancement in enhancing collaboration. These systems analyze student performance data to identify knowledge gaps and personalize learning pathways. By integrating collaborative features, such as peer tutoring sessions or group problem-solving tasks, AI can foster a sense of community among learners. This collaborative approach not only aids in knowledge retention but also builds essential social skills, preparing students for future collaborative endeavors in their academic and professional lives.

Virtual reality (VR) integration in classrooms presents unique opportunities for collaborative learning experiences. AI can enhance VR environments by simulating complex scenarios where students must work together to solve problems or complete projects. For instance, students can engage in immersive simulations that require teamwork, critical thinking, and creative problem-solving. These experiences are enriched with AI-generated feedback, allowing students to reflect on their collaborative processes and outcomes, thus deepening their understanding of group dynamics in real-world contexts.

The ethical implications of AI in educational collaboration cannot be overlooked. As educators and administrators adopt these technologies, they must ensure that their use promotes equity and inclusiveness in learning environments. This involves not only addressing data privacy concerns but also actively working to mitigate biases inherent in AI algorithms. By establishing clear policies and ethical guidelines surrounding AI applications in education, stakeholders can foster a culture of collaboration that prioritizes the well-being and success of all students.

Finally, the ongoing research into AI tools for collaboration in education is essential for understanding their impact and effectiveness. Continuous evaluation of these tools can inform best practices and guide future developments in AI technology. Collaborating with researchers can lead to innovative solutions that enhance educational outcomes, ensuring that AI serves as a valuable ally in fostering collaborative learning environments. By leveraging AI tools thoughtfully and ethically, educators can revolutionize the collaborative experiences of their students, ultimately enriching the educational landscape.

Evaluating the Impact of AI on Group Learning Dynamics

The integration of Artificial Intelligence (AI) into educational settings has significantly transformed group learning dynamics, creating new opportunities and challenges for educators, administrators, and researchers. AI-powered tools and platforms facilitate personalized learning experiences, allowing students to engage with content at their own pace while fostering collaboration among peers. These systems analyze individual learning patterns and adapt group interactions, enhancing the overall educational experience. As a result, understanding the impact of AI on group learning dynamics is crucial for stakeholders aiming to optimize educational outcomes.

One of the primary ways AI influences group learning is through its ability to tailor instruction to diverse learning needs. For instance, AI-driven platforms can assess students' strengths and weaknesses, forming balanced groups that promote collaborative learning. This data-driven approach enables educators to create more effective learning environments where students can support one another, share knowledge, and tackle complex problems collectively. By facilitating meaningful interactions among students, AI enhances engagement and motivation, leading to improved academic performance.

Moreover, AI technologies, such as virtual reality (VR) and augmented reality (AR), introduce immersive experiences that enhance group learning. These tools allow students to explore subjects beyond traditional boundaries, providing a shared platform for collaboration. For example, VR simulations can place students in realistic scenarios where they must work together to solve problems, fostering teamwork and communication skills. This shared experience not only deepens their understanding of the subject matter but also strengthens their ability to collaborate effectively, preparing them for real-world challenges.

However, the integration of AI into group learning also raises ethical considerations and challenges. Issues surrounding data privacy, algorithmic bias, and transparency must be addressed to ensure equitable access to AI resources. Educators and administrators must navigate these complexities, establishing policies that protect student data while leveraging AI's potential to enhance learning. Additionally, ongoing research is essential to evaluate the long-term effects of AI on group dynamics, ensuring that these technologies are implemented responsibly and effectively.

In conclusion, evaluating the impact of AI on group learning dynamics offers valuable insights into the future of education. By harnessing the power of AI in collaborative learning environments, educators can create more personalized, engaging, and effective educational experiences. However, it is essential to remain vigilant about the ethical implications and challenges presented by these technologies. Through thoughtful implementation and continuous evaluation, stakeholders can leverage AI to revolutionize group learning and ultimately enhance educational outcomes for all students.

Chapter 6: The Future of Generative AI in Education

Emerging Trends and Technologies

Emerging trends and technologies in generative AI are reshaping the educational landscape, offering unprecedented opportunities for personalized learning experiences. One of the most significant developments is the rise of AI-powered tutoring systems. These platforms leverage advanced algorithms to analyze student performance data and provide tailored feedback, enabling learners to progress at their own pace. This individualized approach not only addresses diverse learning styles but also helps educators identify areas where students may need additional support. As these systems continue to evolve, they are likely to become integral components of blended learning environments, enhancing traditional instructional methods.

Virtual reality (VR) integration in classrooms represents another transformative trend fueled by generative AI. By combining immersive experiences with AI capabilities, educators can create engaging learning environments that foster deeper understanding of complex subjects. For instance, students can explore historical events or scientific concepts in a 3D space, facilitating experiential learning that traditional methods often lack. Furthermore, AI can adapt VR scenarios based on real-time student interactions, ensuring that each learner receives a customized experience that aligns with their individual needs and interests. This dynamic interplay between AI and VR promises to redefine the ways in which knowledge is imparted and retained.

The ethical implications and policy considerations surrounding AI in education are increasingly coming to the forefront as these technologies advance. Educators and administrators must navigate concerns related to data privacy, algorithmic bias, and the potential for over-reliance on technology. Establishing clear guidelines and frameworks is essential to ensure that AI applications in education serve to enhance learning without compromising ethical standards. Engaging in discussions about AI ethics can help stakeholders develop a shared understanding of the responsibilities associated with implementing these technologies, ultimately fostering a more equitable educational landscape.

Collaborative learning platforms utilizing AI are emerging as effective tools for promoting teamwork and peer-to-peer interaction among students. These platforms harness the power of generative AI to facilitate group projects, enabling students to collaborate seamlessly, regardless of geographical barriers. By providing real-time feedback and monitoring group dynamics, AI can help educators guide students in developing essential skills such as communication and problem-solving. As collaborative learning becomes increasingly important in a globalized world, AI-enhanced platforms will likely play a pivotal role in preparing students for future challenges.

In conclusion, the intersection of generative AI and education is marked by a multitude of emerging trends and technologies that promise to revolutionize teaching and learning practices. As AI-powered tutoring systems, virtual reality integration, ethical considerations, and collaborative platforms continue to evolve, educators, administrators, and researchers must stay informed and adaptable. Embracing these changes will not only enrich the educational experience for students but also empower educators to provide more effective and inclusive learning environments. The future of education is being shaped by these innovations, and a proactive approach is essential for maximizing their potential.

Predictions for the Next Decade

The next decade promises to usher in transformative changes in educational landscapes through the integration of generative AI technologies. As educators, administrators, and researchers, it is essential to anticipate these developments to effectively adapt pedagogical approaches. Generative AI will likely enhance personalized learning experiences by analyzing individual student needs and preferences, allowing for tailored content delivery. This personalized engagement can significantly improve student motivation and learning outcomes, creating a more responsive educational environment.

AI-powered tutoring systems are expected to evolve significantly, leveraging generative AI to provide real-time feedback and adaptive learning pathways. These systems will analyze students' interactions, identifying gaps in knowledge and suggesting resources or exercises to address those needs. This evolution could lead to a shift in the role of educators, who will increasingly become facilitators of learning rather than mere providers of information. The emphasis will be on guiding students through complex problem-solving processes while AI handles the intricacies of personalized content delivery.

The integration of virtual reality (VR) and AI within classrooms will likely redefine experiential learning. As generative AI becomes more sophisticated, it will enable the creation of immersive learning environments that adapt to students' actions and decisions. This will not only enhance engagement but also allow learners to experiment in safe, controlled settings. The use of VR, powered by generative AI, could facilitate collaborative projects, where students from diverse backgrounds work together on shared tasks, enriching their learning experience through global perspectives.

While the potential benefits of generative AI in education are significant, ethical considerations and policy frameworks will become increasingly vital in the next decade. Issues surrounding data privacy, algorithmic bias, and the digital divide will require careful examination and regulation. Educational leaders must advocate for transparent policies that protect student information while ensuring equitable access to AI resources. By prioritizing ethical standards in the deployment of AI technologies, educators can foster a more inclusive and fair educational environment.

Collaborative learning platforms utilizing AI are anticipated to flourish, enabling students to work together across various locations and time zones. These platforms will harness generative AI to facilitate communication, project management, and resource sharing among students. As collaboration becomes more integral to the learning process, educators will need to focus on developing skills that promote teamwork and problem-solving in digital spaces. The next decade offers a unique opportunity to harness the power of generative AI to create a more connected, equitable, and effective educational system.

Preparing Educators for AI-Driven Classrooms

Preparing educators for AI-driven classrooms necessitates a multifaceted approach that encompasses training, resources, and ongoing support. As generative AI technologies evolve, the role of educators must also adapt to integrate these tools effectively into their teaching practices. Professional development programs should focus on understanding AI capabilities, including AI-powered tutoring systems and collaborative learning platforms. By equipping educators with the necessary knowledge and skills, they can harness AI to enhance student engagement, personalize learning experiences, and foster critical thinking.

A critical component of preparing educators is offering comprehensive training on the ethical implications of AI in education. As AI becomes more prevalent, educators must be aware of issues such as data privacy, algorithmic bias, and the potential for inequitable access to technology. Professional development workshops should include discussions on AI ethics and policy, enabling educators to navigate these challenges responsibly. This understanding is crucial not only for the protection of students but also for promoting an inclusive educational environment that values diversity and fairness.

Integrating virtual reality (VR) and AI into classrooms presents unique opportunities and challenges for educators. Professional development should emphasize the practical application of these technologies in lesson planning and classroom management. Educators need training on how to create immersive learning experiences that leverage AI to adapt content to individual student needs. By familiarizing themselves with the technical aspects and pedagogical strategies of VR and AI integration, educators can create engaging and effective learning environments that stimulate students' curiosity and creativity.

Collaboration among educators is essential in the transition to AI-driven classrooms. Establishing collaborative learning platforms utilizing AI can foster peer-to-peer support and resource sharing. Educators can benefit from sharing best practices, lesson plans, and experiences related to AI implementation. Schools and districts should create communities of practice that encourage dialogue and collaboration on AI technologies, allowing educators to learn from each other and collectively develop innovative approaches to teaching and learning.

Finally, ongoing support and resources are vital for sustaining educators' engagement with AI-driven classrooms. This includes access to updated materials, technical support, and regular opportunities for professional development. Educational institutions should prioritize the continuous improvement of their faculty's AI competencies, ensuring that educators remain informed about the latest advancements in generative AI. By fostering a culture of lifelong learning, educators can stay adept in their teaching practices, ultimately enhancing the educational experiences they provide to their students.

Chapter 7: Conclusion and Recommendations

Key Takeaways from the Book

The book "Generative AI: Revolutionizing Educational Experiences" presents several key insights that hold immense relevance for educators, administrators, and researchers in the field of education. One of the primary takeaways is the transformative potential of generative AI in personalizing learning experiences. By leveraging AI algorithms, educational institutions can create adaptive learning environments that respond to individual student needs, learning styles, and paces. This adaptability not only enhances student engagement but also improves retention and understanding of complex concepts, making learning more effective.

Another significant takeaway is the role of AI-powered tutoring systems in providing tailored support to students. These systems can analyze a student's performance in real time and offer immediate feedback and resources that align with their specific challenges. This instant accessibility to personalized assistance can bridge learning gaps and ensure that no student is left behind, particularly in diverse classrooms where learners may have varying levels of preparedness. The integration of such systems into traditional pedagogies fosters a more inclusive educational landscape.

The book also emphasizes the integration of virtual reality and AI in classrooms, showcasing how this combination can create immersive learning experiences. By using virtual environments, students can engage in simulations that enhance their understanding of real-world applications, particularly in subjects like science and history. These experiences not only bolster engagement but also encourage critical thinking and problem-solving skills. Educators are encouraged to explore innovative ways to incorporate these technologies, which can lead to more dynamic and interactive lessons.

Ethics and policy considerations surrounding the use of AI in education are critical topics addressed in the book. As generative AI continues to evolve, it is essential for educational stakeholders to establish ethical guidelines that govern its use. This involves addressing concerns related to data privacy, bias in AI algorithms, and the implications of AI on student autonomy and learning experiences. The book advocates for a collaborative approach in developing policies that both harness the benefits of AI and protect the rights of students, ensuring a balanced integration of technology in education.

Lastly, the book highlights the importance of collaborative learning platforms that utilize AI to foster teamwork and communication among students. These platforms can facilitate group projects, peer reviews, and collaborative problem-solving, enhancing social learning and community building within educational settings. By enabling students to work together in innovative ways, educators can cultivate essential skills such as collaboration, communication, and critical thinking. This shift towards collaborative learning not only prepares students for future workplace demands but also enriches the overall educational experience.

Strategies for Implementation in Educational Settings

Implementing generative AI in educational settings requires a strategic approach that addresses the diverse needs of educators, students, and administrators. One of the primary strategies is to establish a clear framework that aligns AI tools with educational goals. This involves identifying specific learning outcomes that generative AI can enhance, such as personalized learning experiences, improved student engagement, and efficient assessment methods. By integrating AI technologies with established curriculum standards and pedagogical practices, educators can ensure that these tools complement rather than disrupt traditional teaching methodologies.

Another crucial strategy is fostering collaboration among educators, administrators, and technology experts. Creating interdisciplinary teams can facilitate the effective integration of generative AI into the classroom. These teams should work together to identify the most appropriate AI tools for their unique educational contexts, focusing on solutions that enhance collaborative learning and support diverse learning styles. Furthermore, involving educators in the design and selection of AI tools promotes a sense of ownership and encourages the adoption of these technologies among teaching staff.

Professional development plays a significant role in the successful implementation of generative AI in education. Institutions must invest in training programs that equip educators with the necessary skills to effectively use AI-powered tutoring systems and other technologies. Workshops, webinars, and hands-on training sessions should be organized to familiarize educators with AI applications, ensuring they understand how to leverage these tools for maximum impact. Additionally, ongoing support and resources should be made available to help educators stay updated on advancements in AI technology and best practices in its application.

Ethical considerations are paramount when implementing AI in educational settings. Developing policies that address privacy, data security, and equitable access to AI tools is essential. Schools and educational institutions must establish guidelines that protect student information while promoting transparency in AI algorithms. Engaging stakeholders in discussions about AI ethics can foster a culture of responsibility and accountability, ensuring that the deployment of AI technologies aligns with the core values of education. This proactive approach can help mitigate potential risks associated with AI integration.

Finally, measuring the effectiveness of AI implementation is crucial for continuous improvement. Educators and administrators should establish metrics to evaluate the impact of generative AI on student learning outcomes, engagement, and overall educational experience. Collecting and analyzing data on these metrics can inform future decisions regarding AI adoption and guide the refinement of strategies and tools. By fostering a culture of reflection and adaptation, educational institutions can ensure that the integration of generative AI not only enhances learning experiences but also aligns with the evolving landscape of education.

Future Research Directions in Generative AI and Education

As generative AI continues to evolve, its implications for education demand rigorous exploration and research. Future research directions should focus on enhancing AI-powered tutoring systems, particularly in personalizing learning experiences. Investigating how generative AI can adaptively modify content delivery based on individual student needs and learning styles is paramount. This includes the development of algorithms capable of assessing student performance in real time and tailoring instructional materials accordingly. Additionally, research should explore the efficacy of these systems in diverse educational settings, including traditional classrooms, online learning environments, and blended models.

The integration of virtual reality (VR) with generative AI presents another significant research avenue. Studies could examine how immersive environments can be enhanced by AI to create more engaging and interactive learning experiences. Research should focus on developing protocols for incorporating AI-generated content into VR simulations and assessing the impact on student learning outcomes. Furthermore, exploring the potential of AI to create adaptive VR scenarios that respond to student actions will be crucial in understanding how to maximize the effectiveness of such technologies in educational contexts.

Ethical considerations surrounding AI in education must also be at the forefront of future research. Investigating the implications of data privacy, bias in AI algorithms, and the transparency of AI decision-making processes will be essential. Researchers should focus on developing frameworks for ethical AI use in educational settings that prioritize student welfare and equity. This includes examining the policies required to govern the use of AI technologies in classrooms and ensuring that educators are equipped to engage with these tools responsibly and effectively.

Collaborative learning platforms utilizing AI offer yet another promising area for investigation. Future research should delve into how generative AI can facilitate collaborative learning experiences among students. This could involve creating AI systems that enhance peer interactions, support group dynamics, and foster collaborative problem-solving. Research should assess the impact of these platforms on student engagement, motivation, and learning outcomes, providing insights into best practices for implementation in various educational environments.

Finally, interdisciplinary approaches that combine insights from psychology, sociology, and technology will be vital in shaping the future of generative AI in education. By fostering collaboration among educators, technologists, and researchers, a more comprehensive understanding of the potential and limitations of AI in educational contexts can be developed. Future research should emphasize the importance of holistic approaches that consider the socio-emotional aspects of learning and the role of AI in shaping educational experiences. This integrated perspective will be essential as the field continues to evolve, ensuring that generative AI serves to enhance, rather than detract from, the educational mission.

Annex A: Real Classroom Case Studies

Elementary School: Ms. Rodriguez's Adaptive Reading Program

Context

Maria Rodriguez teaches 3rd grade at Lincoln Elementary, a public school serving a diverse population including 40% English Language Learners. Her class of 28 students showed wide variance in reading abilities, making individualized instruction challenging.

Implementation

Ms. Rodriguez implemented an AI-powered reading platform called "LiteracyGrow" that:

- Assessed each student's reading level through an initial diagnostic
- Provided personalized reading materials based on interests and ability
- Offered real-time pronunciation feedback using speech recognition
- Generated comprehension questions tailored to each student's level

Challenges Faced

- Limited devices (only 8 tablets for the classroom)
- Initial parent concerns about screen time and data privacy
- Students needing guidance on using the platform independently
- Integrating AI-assisted reading with traditional classroom activities

Solutions Developed

- Created a rotation schedule for device access
- Hosted a parent night to demonstrate the tool and address privacy concerns
- Implemented a "tech buddy" system pairing tech-savvy students with peers
- Developed 15-minute daily routines that integrated AI feedback into reading groups

Outcomes

After one semester:

- Reading fluency improved by an average of 35% across the class
- Students spent 27% more time voluntarily reading
- The achievement gap between native English speakers and ELL students narrowed
- Ms. Rodriguez reported using the AI-generated insights during parent conferences to provide specific feedback

Reflections

"What surprised me most was how the AI helped me identify patterns I hadn't noticed," notes Ms. Rodriguez. "For example, several students were struggling with the same phonemic awareness skills, which allowed me to create targeted small group instruction. The technology didn't replace my teaching—it enhanced it by giving me better information to work with."

High School: Mr. Chang's AI-Enhanced Physics Lab

Context

James Chang teaches AP Physics at Westridge High School, where limited lab equipment and safety concerns restricted the types of experiments students could perform.

Implementation

Mr. Chang implemented "PhysicsAI Lab," a system combining:

- Virtual reality simulations of dangerous or expensive experiments
- AI-generated experimental variables customized to each student's learning progress
- Real-time feedback on experimental design and execution
- Collaborative virtual workspaces for student teams

Challenges Faced

- High initial cost of VR headsets
- Technical difficulties with calibration and setup
- Student distraction and novelty effect of VR
- Aligning virtual experiments with AP curriculum requirements

Solutions Developed

- Secured funding through a district technology grant and local business partnership
- Established a student "tech team" for troubleshooting and peer support
- Created structured worksheets to focus student attention in VR
- Collaborated with the software developer to create custom AP-aligned modules

Outcomes

- Students performed twice as many experiments as previous years
- Test scores improved by 14% on experimental design questions
- 93% of students reported increased confidence in laboratory skills
- Three female students cited the VR physics experience as influencing their decision to pursue STEM majors

Reflections

"The AI component was key to making this more than just 'cool tech,'" Mr. Chang explains. "The system tracked how students approached problems and adjusted the complexity based on their conceptual understanding. I could see which students needed help with mathematical formulations versus physical intuition. Most importantly, students who were typically hesitant in the physical lab felt more comfortable experimenting in VR, where mistakes didn't mean broken equipment or safety issues."

Middle School: Team-Teaching with AI Assistant

Context

A team of 6th grade teachers at Oakwood Middle School implemented an AI teaching assistant called "EduHelper" across their core curriculum classes to help manage differentiated instruction for 120 students.

Implementation

The teaching team used the AI assistant to:

- Generate differentiated worksheets and activities at three ability levels
- Provide automated feedback on basic writing assignments
- Create customized review materials before assessments
- Facilitate collaborative group formation based on complementary skills

Challenges Faced

- Inconsistent quality of AI-generated materials
- Teacher discomfort with changing roles and workflows
- Student attempts to "game" the AI feedback system
- Balancing AI assistance with developing student self-reliance

Solutions Developed

- Established a quality review process for AI-generated content
- Dedicated professional development time for teacher collaboration and adaptation
- Created clear guidelines for students about appropriate AI use
- Designed "AI-free" assignments to ensure independent skill development

Outcomes

- Teachers reported saving 7+ hours weekly on material preparation
- Student assignment completion rates increased by 23%
- Struggling students showed greater improvement when using AI-scaffolded materials
- Teachers reported more time for one-on-one student interaction

Reflections

"Initially, I feared the AI would make us lazy or less essential," admits Josh Stevens, the team's math teacher. "What actually happened was the opposite—it handled the time-consuming task of creating varied practice materials, which freed us to work directly with students who needed us most. We had to learn to be good editors of the AI's work rather than creators of everything from scratch. The key was maintaining our professional judgment about what students needed while leveraging the AI for efficiency."

Rural District: Ms. Patel's Virtual Expert Network

Context

Deepa Patel teaches high school biology in a rural district with limited resources and no budget for field trips or guest speakers. Many students had never met a working scientist.

Implementation

Ms. Patel used "Expert Connect," an AI platform that:

- Generated lifelike simulations of experts in various scientific fields
- Allowed students to interview "virtual scientists" about career paths and research
- Created customized expert interactions based on student interests
- Provided accurate, curriculum-aligned information through conversational AI

Challenges Faced

- Initial student skepticism about the "fake experts"
- Unreliable rural internet connectivity
- Ensuring AI representations were diverse and culturally sensitive
- Balancing virtual interactions with traditional learning

Solutions Developed

- Paired virtual experts with video lectures from real scientists

- Created downloadable offline versions of core content

- Worked with developers to ensure diverse representation in the AI experts

- Integrated expert interviews with tangible classroom projects

Outcomes

- Student reports showed 78% increased interest in scientific careers

- College application essays frequently referenced insights from virtual experts

- Students initiated a science club to explore topics introduced by AI experts

- Three students secured summer internships after following up on resources mentioned by virtual experts

Reflections

"What made this work wasn't just the technology, but how it opened doors my students thought were closed to them," says Ms. Patel. "One student told me she never considered marine biology because she'd never met anyone in that field—living in a landlocked rural area made it seem impossible. After multiple conversations with the virtual marine biologist and exploring the recommended resources, she's now applying to oceanography programs. The AI experts weren't just information sources; they were possibility models."

Special Education: Mr. Gonzalez's Communication Breakthrough

Context

Eduardo Gonzalez works with non-verbal autistic students at Riverview School. Traditional communication methods had limited success with several students.

Implementation

Mr. Gonzalez implemented "VoiceConnect," an AI communication system that:

- Interpreted subtle physical cues to suggest possible communication intent
- Learned individual student patterns to improve prediction accuracy
- Offered multiple communication modalities (text, symbols, voice)
- Adapted its interface based on student interaction patterns

Challenges Faced

- High variation in student responses to the technology
- Ensuring the AI didn't misinterpret or oversimplify student intent
- Training the AI to recognize individual student communication patterns
- Balancing technology use with developing independent communication skills

Solutions Developed

- Created individual calibration periods for each student
- Established clear protocols for verifying AI interpretations
- Kept detailed logs of successful and unsuccessful interactions for AI training
- Developed a gradual reduction plan as students developed more independent communication

Outcomes

- Two non-verbal students began consistently expressing preferences and needs
- Classroom disruptions decreased by 62% as communication improved
- Parents reported using similar communication techniques at home with positive results
- Three students transitioned to simplified versions of the technology with increased independence

Reflections

"The technology wasn't perfect," Mr. Gonzalez acknowledges, "but it gave us a starting point when we had been at an impasse. The key insight was that the AI could detect patterns in student behavior that might indicate communication intent before it was obvious to human observers. This early detection allowed us to respond more consistently to communication attempts, which encouraged more attempts. It became a positive cycle of reinforcement."

Annex B: Student Perspectives on AI in Education

Elementary School Voices

Jamal, 9 years old, 3rd grade "I used to hate reading time because I always got stuck on hard words. Now I read with Robot Buddy [AI reading assistant], and when I don't know a word, I can ask it for help without everyone hearing me get it wrong. The robot shows me how to sound it out and remembers which words I need help with. Yesterday I finished a whole chapter book by myself!"

Sofia, 10 years old, 4th grade "Math used to make me cry because when I didn't understand something, the class would move on anyway. Now we use MathMaster [AI math program], and it gives me extra practice on fractions because it knows I'm still confused. It doesn't make me feel dumb when I get something wrong. My teacher says I've improved a lot, and now I sometimes help other kids."

Tyler, 8 years old, 2nd grade "The storytelling robot is my favorite! It asks me questions about what characters I want and what should happen in the story, then it makes a book with me in it! My mom put one of our stories on the fridge. I wrote some parts and the computer helped with other parts."

Teacher observation from Ms. Williams: "What's fascinating is how the AI has changed peer dynamics. Students who previously hid their struggles now openly discuss strategy with peers because the AI has normalized the idea that everyone learns differently. They'll say things like 'the AI told me I need to practice this more' without embarrassment."

Middle School Perspectives

Marcus, 12 years old, 7th grade "At first I thought the AI writing coach was going to be like spell-check, boring and annoying. But it actually helps me think better. When I'm stuck, it asks me questions about what I want to say next or suggests ways to make my point stronger. My history essay got an A because the AI helped me organize my arguments better. It didn't write it for me—it just helped me figure out what I wanted to say."

Ava, 13 years old, 8th grade "I thought science was just memorizing facts until we started using the AI lab simulations. Now we can design experiments that would be too dangerous in real life, like testing chemical reactions. The AI gives us hints when we're missing something important but doesn't just give us the answers. Last week my team figured out how to create a more efficient solar cell design, and it felt like being a real scientist."

Devon, 11 years old, 6th grade "Sometimes I get distracted easily, but the AI system knows this and sends me little reminders to focus. It's not annoying like when a teacher calls you out in front of everyone. The AI shows me how long I've been focused and gives me points for staying on task. My concentration has gotten a lot better, and my parents are really proud."

From student journal entry: "The weird thing about having an AI tutor is that I don't feel embarrassed asking 'stupid' questions. Last year I would never raise my hand because I was afraid everyone would think I wasn't smart. Now I can ask the AI anything, and it never makes me feel bad. This has actually made me more confident about speaking up in class too."

High School Insights

Zoe, 16 years old, 11th grade "The college counseling AI changed everything for me. My parents didn't go to college, so they couldn't help me with the process. The AI helped me find scholarships I never would have discovered and guided me through application essays. It even connected me with virtual mentors in my field of interest. I got accepted to three universities with scholarships, and I don't think that would have happened without this support."

Jason, 17 years old, 12th grade "I was skeptical about the AI debate partner in our civics class, but it's actually made me a better thinker. It can argue both sides of any issue really well, which helps me see weaknesses in my own arguments. Sometimes I think I have an unbeatable point, and then the AI shows me a perspective I hadn't considered. Our teacher says the quality of class discussions has improved dramatically."

Mia, 15 years old, 10th grade "The AI creativity assistant in art class is controversial. Some students think it's cheating to use AI for art, but our teacher encourages us to see it as a collaboration tool. I use it to explore different styles or techniques I couldn't execute on my own yet. Then I learn from what it shows me and try to develop those skills myself. It's like having an expert looking over your shoulder, suggesting possibilities."

Miguel, 18 years old, 12th grade "As someone with dyslexia, the AI tools have leveled the playing field for me. The text-to-speech and speech-to-text features mean I can focus on my ideas instead of struggling with reading and writing mechanics. The AI also formats my papers automatically according to MLA or APA guidelines, which used to take me hours to figure out. My grades reflect my actual understanding now, not my disability."

College Student Reflections

Aisha, 19 years old, freshman "The transition to college was overwhelming until I started using the AI study assistant. It analyzes my course materials and creates personalized study guides that focus on my weak areas. It also helps me plan my study schedule around my other commitments. My first-semester GPA was much higher than I expected."

Elijah, 21 years old, junior "I have mixed feelings about AI in education. In my computer science program, we use AI coding assistants that make programming much more accessible. But sometimes I worry that I'm becoming dependent on the AI suggestions rather than developing my own problem-solving skills. The best professors limit AI use for foundational concepts but allow it for more complex projects."

Priya, 20 years old, sophomore "The research assistant AI has transformed how I write papers. Instead of spending hours searching for relevant sources, the AI can suggest peer-reviewed articles based on my thesis statement. It also helps me identify gaps in my argument or places where I need more evidence. The key is using it to enhance my thinking, not replace it."

From a student focus group: "The ethical discussions about AI have been the most valuable part of the experience. Our philosophy class debates whether AI-assisted work should be disclosed, who owns AI-human collaborative creations, and how these tools might widen or narrow educational disparities. These conversations prepare us for a world where AI will be part of every professional field."

Insights Across Age Groups

Common Themes from Student Feedback:

1. **Reduced anxiety**: Students consistently report feeling less stressed about making mistakes when working with AI tools that offer private feedback.
2. **Personalized pacing**: The ability to move faster or slower through material without holding back peers or falling behind was mentioned by students of all ages.
3. **Increased agency**: Students appreciate having more control over their learning process and the ability to direct their own exploration.
4. **Enhanced creativity**: Many students describe using AI tools to overcome creative blocks or explore new possibilities.
5. **Changing relationship with teachers**: Students note that teachers spend less time delivering content and more time providing mentorship and personalized guidance.
6. **Concerns about authenticity**: Older students especially express concerns about defining "original work" in an AI-assisted learning environment.
7. **Digital literacy development**: Students recognize they're developing critical skills in evaluating AI outputs and using AI tools effectively.
8. **Accessibility benefits**: Students with learning differences particularly value how AI tools can provide alternative access paths to educational content.

Educator Insights on Student Experiences:

"What's most striking in these student perspectives is the shift from passive to active learning," notes Dr. Elena Vasquez, educational psychologist. "When students describe their experiences with AI tools, they use language of partnership and collaboration rather than consumption. This active engagement with the learning process may be as important as any specific content knowledge they gain."

Annex C: Resource List: AI Tools for Educators

This curated collection focuses on practical, accessible AI tools that educators can implement in various learning environments. Each listing includes pricing information, technical requirements, implementation difficulty, and best practices for educational use.

Reading and Language Arts

1. ReadFlow AI

Description: Adaptive reading platform that adjusts text complexity based on student reading level while maintaining content relevance. Includes comprehension checks and vocabulary building.

Grade Levels: 2-12

Pricing: Free basic version; $5/student/year for premium features

Technical Requirements: Works on any web browser; tablets recommended for younger students

Implementation Difficulty: ⭐⭐ (Moderate)

Best Practices:

- Begin with short reading sessions (15 minutes) to acclimate students
- Use the teacher dashboard to identify common vocabulary gaps across the class
- Integrate with writing activities by having students respond to AI-selected texts

2. VoiceScribe

Description: Speech-to-text and text-to-speech platform with feedback on pronunciation, fluency, and expression. Supports multiple languages.

Grade Levels: K-12

Pricing: Free for basic features; $8/student/month for advanced feedback

Technical Requirements: Requires microphone access; works best with headsets

Implementation Difficulty: ★★★ (Challenging for younger students)

Best Practices:

- Create speaking/listening centers in elementary classrooms
- For ELL students, pair with visual supports
- Use recording features to track progress over time

3. StoryForge

Description: AI-assisted creative writing platform that provides prompts, character development suggestions, and feedback on narrative structure.

Grade Levels: 3-12

Pricing: Free for teachers; premium features $3/student/month

Technical Requirements: Web-based; compatible with all devices

Implementation Difficulty: ★ (Easy)

Best Practices:

- Begin with collaborative stories before individual projects
- Use the "story starters" feature for students with writing reluctance
- Enable the "feedback mode" that suggests improvements rather than corrections

Mathematics

4. MathMentor AI

Description: Adaptive math practice platform that identifies knowledge gaps and creates personalized learning pathways with real-time feedback.

Grade Levels: 1-12

Pricing: Free trial; $7/student/month or district pricing available

Technical Requirements: Works on any internet-connected device

Implementation Difficulty: ★★ (Moderate)

Best Practices:

- Use diagnostic assessments at beginning of units
- Review weekly AI-generated progress reports to inform instruction
- Supplement with hands-on activities for concepts students find challenging

5. GeometryVision

Description: AR/VR geometry exploration tool with AI guidance that helps students visualize and manipulate 3D shapes.

Grade Levels: 6-12

Pricing: $12/student/year; school licenses available

Technical Requirements: Tablets or VR headsets; can work with basic web version

Implementation Difficulty: ★★★ (Requires technical setup)

Best Practices:

- Begin with guided whole-class explorations
- Pair with physical manipulatives for conceptual reinforcement
- Use the recording feature to have students explain their spatial reasoning

6. AlgebraCoach

Description: Step-by-step algebra problem solver with customizable hints and explanations that adapt to student error patterns.

Grade Levels: 7-12

Pricing: Free basic version; $6/student/month for advanced features

Technical Requirements: Web-based; works on all devices

Implementation Difficulty: ★ (Easy)

Best Practices:

- Use "explain mode" to focus on process rather than answers
- Assign specific problem sets that align with classroom instruction
- Have students create their own problems for peers to solve

Science

7. LabSimulate

Description: Virtual science laboratory with AI guidance that allows students to conduct experiments too dangerous, expensive, or time-consuming for physical classrooms.

Grade Levels: 5-12

Pricing: Free basic simulations; $15/student/year for full access

Technical Requirements: Works best on tablets or computers; limited functionality on smartphones

Implementation Difficulty: ★★ (Moderate)

Best Practices:

- Pair virtual labs with physical demonstrations when possible
- Use the prediction feature before running simulations
- Have students document observations in lab notebooks, not just digital responses

8. EcoSystem Builder

Description: AI-powered ecosystem simulation that allows students to create and modify environments, introducing variables and observing outcomes.

Grade Levels: 4-12

Pricing: $9/student/year; free trial available

Technical Requirements: Requires updated browsers with WebGL support

Implementation Difficulty: ★★ (Moderate)

Best Practices:

- Start with guided ecosystems before open exploration
- Connect to local environmental issues when possible
- Use the time-acceleration feature to observe long-term changes

9. GeneticExplorer

Description: Genetics simulation with AI guidance that visualizes heredity concepts and allows exploration of genetic engineering principles.

Grade Levels: 8-12

Pricing: $11/student/year

Technical Requirements: Works on any internet-connected device

Implementation Difficulty: ★★★ (Complex concepts require teacher facilitation)

Best Practices:

- Begin with basic inheritance models before complex simulations

- Use the comparative visualization tools to track genetic changes

- Incorporate ethical discussions alongside technical explorations

Social Studies and History

10. TimeTravel Interviews

Description: AI-simulated historical figures that students can interview, with responses based on historical records and primary sources.

Grade Levels: 4-12

Pricing: $7/student/year; discounts for school-wide adoption

Technical Requirements: Works on any internet-connected device

Implementation Difficulty: ★ (Easy)

Best Practices:

- Have students prepare questions in advance

- Compare AI responses to primary source documents

- Use as introduction to research projects

11. GeoCulture Explorer

Description: Interactive cultural geography platform with AI guides that introduce students to global perspectives and cultural practices.

Grade Levels: 3-12

Pricing: Free basic version; $5/student/year for premium features

Technical Requirements: Works best on tablets or computers with audio capabilities

Implementation Difficulty: ★★ (Moderate)

Best Practices:

- Connect explorations to current events when appropriate
- Pair with authentic cultural exchanges when possible
- Use comparison features to highlight cultural similarities and differences

12. CivicSimulate

Description: Government and civics simulation that uses AI to model outcomes of policy decisions and electoral processes.

Grade Levels: 8-12

Pricing: $10/student/year

Technical Requirements: Works on any internet-connected device

Implementation Difficulty: ★★★ (Requires background knowledge)

Best Practices:

- Begin with structured scenarios before open simulations
- Use decision points to foster debate and discussion
- Compare simulation outcomes to real-world examples

Special Education and Accessibility

13. AdaptLearn

Description: Comprehensive learning platform with AI adaptation for diverse learning needs, including dyslexia, ADHD, and autism spectrum supports.

Grade Levels: K-12

Pricing: $14/student/year; often eligible for special education funding

Technical Requirements: Works on any device; compatible with screen readers

Implementation Difficulty: ★★ (Requires initial customization)

Best Practices:

- Work with special education teams to optimize individual settings
- Regularly review adaptation effectiveness and adjust
- Use data insights to inform IEP goals and progress monitoring

14. CommunicateAI

Description: Communication support tool for non-verbal and speech-challenged students that predicts communication intent and offers symbol-based or text options.

Grade Levels: Pre-K-12

Pricing: $18/student/year; often covered by assistive technology funding

Technical Requirements: Works best on tablets with touchscreens

Implementation Difficulty: ★★★ (Requires personalized setup)

Best Practices:

- Begin with high-interest topics to encourage engagement

- Involve speech therapists in implementation planning

- Create consistent opportunities for communication throughout the day

15. FocusAssist

Description: Attention management tool that uses AI to identify optimal learning periods and provide personalized focus strategies.

Grade Levels: 3-12

Pricing: $8/student/year

Technical Requirements: Works on any device; optional wearable integration

Implementation Difficulty: ★★ (Requires routine establishment)

Best Practices:

- Teach metacognitive awareness alongside tool use

- Start with shorter focus sessions and build duration

- Review patterns with students to develop self-regulation strategies

Teacher Tools

16. LessonCraft AI

Description: Lesson planning assistant that generates differentiated activities, assessments, and resources based on learning objectives.

Grade Levels: K-12

Pricing: $15/month per teacher; school licenses available

Technical Requirements: Web-based; works on any device

Implementation Difficulty: ⭐ (Intuitive interface)

Best Practices:

- Use as a starting point, then customize for your specific students
- Develop template lessons for recurring instructional formats
- Utilize the differentiation features to create tiered activities

17. GradeAssist

Description: AI-powered assessment tool that provides initial feedback on written assignments and suggests targeted comments.

Grade Levels: 3-12

Pricing: $10/month per teacher; district pricing available

Technical Requirements: Works on any internet-connected device

Implementation Difficulty: ⭐⭐ (Requires calibration to grading style)

Best Practices:

- Review and personalize all AI suggestions before sharing with students
- Use time saved to provide more detailed feedback on complex aspects
- Share rubrics with the AI system to improve alignment

18. DataInsight Educator

Description: Learning analytics platform that identifies patterns in student performance and suggests intervention strategies.

Grade Levels: K-12

Pricing: $12/student/year with volume discounts

Technical Requirements: Integrates with most LMS systems

Implementation Difficulty: ★★★ (Requires data integration)

Best Practices:

- Focus on actionable insights rather than just data collection
- Share appropriate analytics with students to support goal-setting
- Use trend identification to adjust instructional approaches mid-unit

Implementation Support Resources

Teacher Communities

- **AI Educators Network**: Free online community with implementation guides and peer support
- **EdTech Innovators Forum**: Monthly webinars on AI integration best practices
- **Classroom AI Alliance**: Resource-sharing platform with lesson plan exchange

Professional Development

- **AI Fundamentals for Educators**: Free 10-hour online course
- **Ethical AI Implementation**: Certificate program offered through multiple universities
- **Student Data Privacy Workshop Series**: Available for district-wide training

Research and Evaluation Tools

- **AI Impact Assessment Framework**: Free downloadable tool for evaluating effectiveness
- **Implementation Rubric**: Guidelines for staged implementation of AI tools
- **Student Feedback Surveys**: Age-appropriate assessment instruments for gathering learner perspectives

Getting Started Guide

First Steps for AI Implementation

1. **Assess needs**: Identify specific challenges in your classroom that AI tools might address
2. **Start small**: Choose one tool in your subject area with manageable technical requirements
3. **Secure permissions**: Review your school's technology policies and obtain necessary approvals
4. **Prepare students**: Introduce the purpose of the AI tool and set clear expectations
5. **Gather feedback**: Regularly check in with students about their experience
6. **Reflect and adjust**: Document successes and challenges to inform future implementation

Avoiding Common Pitfalls

- **Technology overload**: Introduce new tools gradually, not all at once
- **Unrealistic expectations**: Understand that AI tools supplement rather than replace good teaching
- **Insufficient training**: Ensure you're comfortable with the tool before introducing it to students
- **Neglecting ethics**: Discuss appropriate use and limitations with students
- **Implementation isolation**: Connect with colleagues implementing similar tools to share insights

Measuring Success

- Focus on specific learning outcomes rather than general technology usage
- Collect both quantitative data (test scores, completion rates) and qualitative feedback
- Compare similar assignments with and without AI support
- Monitor changes in student engagement and attitudes toward subject matter
- Track time savings and how that time is reinvested in other instructional activities

www.ingramcontent.com/pod-product-compliance
Lightning Source LLC
Chambersburg PA
CBHW080602060326
40689CB00021B/4911

* 9 7 9 8 2 8 0 4 9 5 1 3 5 *